Andrew and Sue make a kite

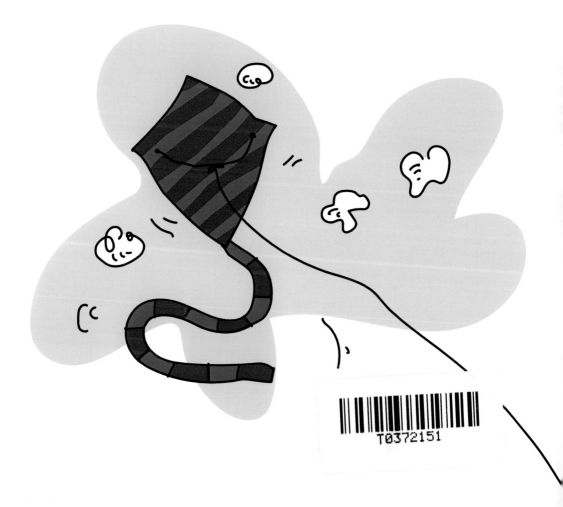

"I would like to make a kite," said Andrew.
"Let's look on the computer and see how to do it," said Sue.
They looked on the computer.

"You read it," said Andrew,
"and tell me what to do."

Sue said, "1: Cut out the kite.
2: Cut out the tail.
3: Get a tube of glue.
4: Glue the kite on the wood.
5: Put the tail on the kite.
6: Glue on a string."

Andrew said, "We could cut up the newspaper. Dad and Mum have finished it."
Andrew drew the kite on the newspaper and did as Sue had said.

Then they looked at the
kite Andrew had made.
"Let me put blue on it,"
said Sue.
"I'll put red on it," said
Andrew. "Then we will
have a blue and red
newspaper kite."

Sue put red and blue on the tail too. They had to wait while the kite dried.

The children went to the park. Andrew threw the kite. Up, up, up it went, into the blue sky.

Andrew flew the kite. He had to run as it swooped up and down, up and down.

"You have a go,"
Andrew said to Sue.

The kite swooped up and down, up and down. Sue had to run and run. It was a lot of fun.

Then CRASH! The kite
flew into a big tree.

Oh dear! Oh dear!
The kite was torn.

"We will glue it and fix it up," said Andrew, "and we will run with it again."

Words to blend

make	kite	go
like	they	read
me	while	dried
sky	we	made
children	looked	newspaper
dear	have	wait

Before reading

Synopsis: Andrew and Sue want to make a kite. They look up on the computer how to make one. They use newspaper and paint it red and blue and it flies!

Review graphemes: ow o-e oe o

Phoneme: oo/oo

New graphemes: ew ue u-e u oul

Story discussion: Look at the cover, and read the title together. Ask: *How do you think Andrew and Sue will make their kite? What could they use? What might happen?* Discuss children's predictions for what might happen in the story.

Link to prior learning: Remind children that the sounds /oo/ as in *good* and as in *food* can also be spelt in lots of other ways. How many can they remember? Display the following words and ask children to sort them according to the way the /oo/ sounds are spelt: *new, glue, tube, should, unicorn, put, could, flute, clue, threw.*

Vocabulary check: Tube – a squeezable container for things like toothpaste and glue. Remind children that the word *tube* can also mean a cylinder shape.

Decoding practice: Ask children to turn to page 5. Challenge them to find three words where the /oo/ sound is spelled *ew* (*Andrew, newspaper, drew*).

Tricky word practice: Display the word *do*. Ask children to circle the tricky part – the letter o, which makes a long /oo/ sound. Encourage children to practise writing this word and look out for this and other words with the same spelling pattern in their reading (e.g. *to*).

After reading

Apply learning: Discuss the story. Ask: *Why do you think Andrew wasn't cross when the kite got broken? What will the children do next, after the story ends?*

Comprehension

- What do Andrew and Sue use to make the kite?

- Where do they find the instructions for the kite?

- How does the kite get broken?

Fluency

- Pick a page that most of the group read quite easily. Ask them to reread it with pace and expression. Model how to do this if necessary.

- In pairs, children can read pages 10 to 11, taking turns to read a sentence each with appropriate expression.

- Practise reading the words on page 17.

Tricky words review

here	said	come
do	you	what
out	have	people
some	oh	was
were	there	called